NON-SMOKER FOR LIFE

NON-SMOKER FOR LIFE

Mary J. Stevens, Ph.D.,
and Harry Alexander

A Hearthstone Book

Carlton Press Corp. New York, NY

Illustrations in Chapter 2 by Robert D. Lowery

Manufactured in the United States of America
ISBN 0-8062-4977-3

CONTENTS

INTRODUCTION
HISTORY OF TOBACCO USE

Before we get to the real meat of the matter, it's important to outline some of the whys and wherefores of smoking. Without this information, you won't be able to make the intelligent decision to give up cigarettes for good. So, settle back in your chair, light up, and take a brief trip through history, with some economics thrown in for good measure, and learn about this "thing" called smoking.

When Sir Walter Raleigh came to the New World in the 17th century, he brought with him something that would forever change the lives of the Native Americans who tried it and the people who would further settle the New World. It was also something that would make a lot of money for future generations. It was tobacco.

Raleigh probably never thought his tobacco plants would produce and cause the health problems that society is faced with today. After all, the main reason for introducing tobacco to the New World was economic. Tobacco was used as a means of trading with the Native Americans. Tobacco was something the people who first inhabited the land didn't have. It was also something that was not widely available in Europe. That made it a prime trading commodity.

Tobacco was also thought to be a cure for a variety of ailments in the European culture dating as far back as the 17th century. There was talk that it would cure headaches, asthma, gout and ulcers. Tobacco was even thought to be a cure for the Black Plague. Some Europeans did find a use for tobacco. But most believed it to be a drug that should be left alone. Jesuit priest Jacob Blade wondered why tobacco should be touted as a cure for anything. He wrote in 1658, "What's the difference between smoking and suicide, except that one takes longer to kill himself than the other?"

In any event, it was found that tobacco could be grown more efficiently in the New World than anywhere else. The climate was right in the colonies of Virginia, North Carolina and South Carolina. The region got the right amount of rainfall each year to produce the crop. Once tobacco was established as a cash crop for the colonists, there was a big call for it in Europe. The colonies were aided in their endeavor by European governments. By the late 19th century, the American tobacco industry was flourishing and any arguments against the use of tobacco were seen as not valid.

It wouldn't be fair though, to blame Raleigh for today's troubles with tobacco. Prior to his mass introduction of the tobacco plant in the New World, smoking did exist. History tells us that, in pre-Columbian times, people smoked substances largely for ceremonial purposes. Indian cultures would smoke a peace pipe to celebrate the end of a battle or to ward off further hostilities. Substances used for smoking were also part of religious ceremonies on the part of Indian cultures.

By the beginning of the 20th century, the tobacco industry was ready to take off. World War I saw cigarette smoking become global. And, while smoking prior to the First World War was a predominate male pursuit, more and more women craved to try it. The tobacco companies saw that as another avenue for their marketing efforts.

Some in the medical profession believed smoking caused health problems, but they were largely in the minority. In the 1930s, medical research started showing a link between smoking and health. More research resulted in further evidence that smoking was bad for a person's health. The first time the U.S. government told us about the dangers of smoking was in a U.S. Surgeon General report released in 1964. It said, among other things, that smoking was habit-forming. Another report from the U.S. Surgeon General in 1979 was more direct. It stated that smoking was the "prototypical substance abuse dependency."

The decade of the 1980s saw the fight to ban tobacco expand. Many communities passed ordinances prohibiting smoking in restaurants, the workplace and other public places. Further studies showed not only smokers were causing themselves health problems. Second-hand smoke generated by the smoker was shown to cause other health problems for other people. The aim of regulation was if people would not take it upon themselves to heed government warnings, then the government would impose guidelines to protect the general health.

So, if all this medical research on the effects of smoking is available for public consumption, why do you continue to smoke? Are you ignoring the facts that smoking is bad for your health and the health of those around you? Probably not. It's that you can't quit the habit for good. You've undoubtedly tried to quit more than once. For that matter, you may be an expert at "stopping" since you've done it so often. The problem is that you have not been able to stay stopped. There are a number of factors that complicate a person's will to stop smoking. Advertising the tobacco product is one. Yes, all the ads you see for cigarettes carry a government warning on the dangers and effects of smoking. But, it's an image thing that's conveyed in the advertising message.

Look closely at an advertisement for cigarettes in your favorite magazine. What does it show? It depicts people, usually upper-class, enjoying a good time while smoking. You can sail and smoke. You can herd cattle while smoking. You can race cars while smoking. The list goes on and on. The advertising industry has created an image of the smoker. Members of the lower socio-economic groups strive to be just like the people they see depicted in the advertisements. Remember the Marlboro Man? For years, Madison Avenue showed us that his image was one that we could achieve. We could smoke and be a big wheel on the range. The Marlboro Man is now herding cattle on that big range in the sky. He died of lung cancer resulting from smoking.

The U.S. government in the 1970s banned tobacco advertising from the broadcast media. But that wasn't accomplished without a fight from the tobacco companies and other tobacco interests. Tobacco advertising is still pervasive in some print media—magazines and billboards, for instance.

As the decade of the '90s dawned, smoking was banned on domestic airline flights of less than three hours. Pipe and cigar smoking had been banned much earlier from the airlines. There's a move now to completely ban cigarette smoking from all airline flights originating in the United States.

What about the effects of second-hand smoke? A U.S. Environmental Protection Agency Report issued in January 1993 stated that second-hand smoke is a carcinogen and it kills an estimated three thousand non-smokers a year from lung cancer. The Centers for Disease Control has also been studying the effects of second-hand smoke. It's study had not been completed as of January 1993. But in preliminary reports, the CDC said it found signs of nicotine in the bodies of those people tested. All told, the CDC is testing 23,000 Americans from age four to ninety-one. The first eight hundred people tested showed traces of cotinine, a by-product of nicotine, in blood serum. The CDC won't have complete results until its study, begun in 1988, is completed sometime in 1994.

Now that you've got an idea about the history of tobacco, let's look at your history with it.

NON-SMOKER FOR LIFE

1.
ADDICTIONS & HABITS

We're intelligent enough to know that smoking is harmful to our health and the health of those around us. Yet we continue to light up. Why? Is it an addiction or is it a habit?

ADDICTION

Think about what happens to you when you light up a cigarette. You can solve all the world's problems while puffing on that cigarette. Or, you seem to take on and complete various tasks and projects while a cigarette is in your hand or mouth. That's because you believe you have the ability to think clearly while inhaling the smoke.

Maybe your overall disposition improves while smoking. Angry? Try lighting up and see what happens. Your humor more than likely will return and chances are you'll forget what it was that you were so angry about, or at least you'll not be as mad. If you're depressed about something, you think that cigarette will help ease the pain and help you think clearer.

That cigarette also allows you to take time out from the daily grind. While puffing away, you don't really have to worry about generating that sales report, do you? It could wait until you put out that butt, right?

Wrong. Those pressures of everyday life are still with you regardless if you smoke one cigarette a day or ten packs in a week's time.

Mental health professionals have a yardstick that they use to determine if an individual is addicted to a psychoactive substance, like nicotine. It's an objective measure, not subjective. The difference is that in an objective study, the evidence is clearly measurable. In a subjective study, the evidence cannot be clearly measured. Instead, it's a study that reports thoughts, feelings and emotions.

It would seem that according to a number of government and private studies, smoking is an addiction, providing a chemical "high." It's not the actual smoking that's causing the addiction, but the nicotine that's contained within the cigarette.

Here's how you can determine for yourself if you're addicted to nicotine. If you say "yes" to at least three of the following statements, you've bought the farm, so to speak:

1. If you're smoking substantially more now than when you started.
2. If you have a persistent desire for a cigarette or have had one or more unsuccessful efforts to cut down or quit smoking.
3. If you spend a lot of time necessary to get the nicotine into your system, i.e., chain smoking.
4. If you've given up going to social events or quit your one-time favorite sport because smoking isn't allowed.
5. If you keep on smoking even though you know it's bad for your health and the health of those around you.
6. If your tolerance level is way up. In other words, it takes more cigarettes to achieve the desired feeling you want.
7. If you smoke a cigarette to avoid the unpleasantness of quitting (withdrawal).

To further illustrate the addiction caused by nicotine, former U.S. Surgeon General C. Everett Koop released a report in 1988 called *The Health Consequences of Smoking: Nicotine Addiction.* Among other things, it came right out and said that the drug in cigarettes—nicotine—is addicting. The report stated that:

> The pharmacological and behavioral processes that determine tobacco addiction are similar to those that determine addiction to drugs such as heroin and cocaine.

Another U.S. Surgeon General report on smoking published in 1986, gave a chilling account about the effects of nicotine addiction:

> These levels of nicotine are substantial, since the relative potency of nicotine is 5 to 10 times greater than that of cocaine in producing discriminate subjective effects (1 to 2 milligrams of nicotine given intravenously, orally, or inhaled, produces reliable, behavioral and physiological effects).

Simply stated, the ability of nicotine to cause a noticeable change in emotions, feelings and behavior is five to ten times greater than that of cocaine.

There's more to the addiction portion of smoking and you've probably read about it in all the newspapers, but there's also the habit side to smoking. Here's a statistic to ponder: If you're a pack-a-day smoker, you've puffed away 75,000 times over the past year. Startled? You shouldn't be, because having practiced that often on something, you ought to be pretty good at it by now. What we aim to do, is to help you change that pattern of behavior.

HABITS

What is a habit? Is it a patterned behavior or one that's learned over time? Actually, it's both. Most psychologists agree that a habit is something that's learned over time. You've heard of Pavlov's dogs? That was a study done by the Russian psychologist Ivan Pavlov in the late 1880s on the unlearned, or relatively automatic reflexes associated with digestion. The upshot of the study was that he saw that dogs sometimes salivated in anticipation of getting food. He believed that action to not be a learned, or conditioned one. In other words, when the dogs saw food, they started salivating. So, he wondered if there was another ways dogs might be conditioned to salivate. He tried a variety of things from ringing a bell to turning on a metronome. As it turned out, those dogs, over a period of time, were conditioned (or learned) to salivate to a number of signals. Well, there are some things in life that have conditioned you to smoke.

The "Pavlovian Bell" automatically rings for you to pick up a cigarette whenever you're in a stressful situation. That's because you have learned that the smoking behavior conditioned you to quiet stress with nicotine for the moment. It also automatically rings for you when you first rise in the morning to have a cup of coffee, or when the telephone rings. Is it possible to carry on a telephone conversation without a cigarette? Yes. The bell continues to ring almost nonstop throughout the day in virtually any activity in which you engage.

Just as you take an aspirin to relieve a headache, you ingest nicotine to make whatever situation you're in go a little easier. Let's explore that further.

Co-author Alexander had smoked almost one pack of cigarettes a day for twenty years.

"I've also been a softball player for as long as I can remember. I had a habit of making sure that I got one last cigarette in before the first pitch of the game. I thought it helped my concentration and I could tune out the jeers of the other team. That last smoke before the game started also helped me remember who hits the ball down the third base line and who tried to hit between me and the shortstop. The way I played the game hinged on if I'd had that smoke before it was time to take the field or step into the batter's box. I knew for a fact that if I had a cigarette before it was my time to hit, I'd be able to hit that elusive home run—the one that I'd been trying to hit for the past twenty-five years. I do know that I was more alert in the game if I'd puffed before the first pitch and my anxiety level about my declining field prowess in growing older went away. I was comfortable with the fact that I'd been able to keep fit and trim because I was a smoker. And, win or lose, the ball game was that much more enjoyable after the last out was recorded because I could light up again."

Funny, all of the above—in maybe a different context—are what all smokers have to say when surveyed on the subject.

2.
THE MYTHS OF QUITTING

IS IT 'WILL POWER' OR 'WON'T POWER?'

Co-author Alexander's father was a smoker for at least twenty-five years.

"He probably smoked a pack a day," says Alexander. "I noticed one day that he no longer smoked. I asked him why. He told me that he decided he could give it up on his own. The man was strong willed in his daily life. I later learned that he suffered from another medical ailment and for him to live longer, he had to give up cigarettes. To this day, I'm not sure if his 'will power' won out or if medical science prevailed in convincing him to quit. There's no question that smoking was a contributing factor to his death. But he had an added problem. He worked in an asbestos plant and constantly inhaled asbestos fibers. It was a combination of those fibers and the carcinogens from the smoke that caused his death."

Co-author Stevens' father was a pipe smoker. She recalls how, as a little girl, she used to watch her father shave, switching his pipe from one corner of his mouth to the other to manage a clean shave. "Pop and I used to like going for walks in the rain. The rain didn't stop his smoking . . . he just turned the bowl of the pipe upside down to keep the tobacco dry. Nothing seemed to interfere with his love affair with his pipe. He lit it immediately following an early breakfast and retired it to the ashtray as he prepared for bed at night. Obviously, nicotine did something special for Pop. It was not until his first heart attack that he tried to become a nonsmoker. After futile attempts to cease and desist he temporarily settled for smoking cigarettes or cigars. It was temporary indeed, for he went right back to his pipe within months. After a second heart attack and hearing the added diagnosis of emphysema, he tried again. He was a bit more successful this time because he was having difficulty breathing and smoking at the same time. (Have you ever had such a bad cold you could barely breathe and still you lit up?) He finally succeeded in retiring his pipe completely and having only an occasional cigarette. Nicotine had its icy, addictive grip on him until his third and fatal heart attack."

There are some who argue that if you have the "will power" to stop smoking, you'll be able to do it. For some, that may work. But consider this: smoking is not only a habit, but the nicotine contained within the cigarette is an addictive drug.

Why does nicotine do all of the things it does to you/ for you?

Well, let's follow some nicotine from that smoke you are inhaling into your body and see what actually happens.

Within seconds of that first puff, pure nicotine is delivered to many nerve cells (neurons) both outside and inside your central nervous system (brain and spinal cord), the communication and control center for the entire body. Nicotine is a chemical transmitter-like substance which is relayed to other nerve cells throughout the body by way of electro-chemical nerve impulses. These impulses are conducted from one end of the nerve to its termination through a series of junctions called synapses. The nerve termination may be a junction with another nerve, a gland or a muscle. Most junctions between nerves operate by the release of chemical substances transmitted from the termination of the first segment of the nerve to specific sites or receptors on the following nerve segment. (Figure 1.)

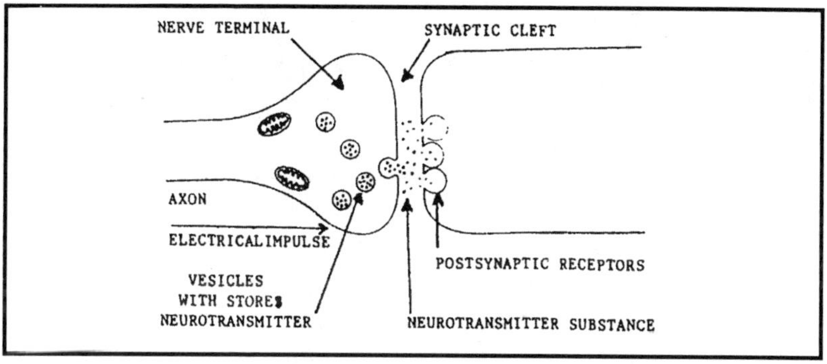

Figure 1. The Synapse

There are at least thirty different true transmitter substances known, but the one in which we are particularly interested is acetylcholine (ACh).

Why acetylcholine in particular? Because nicotine mimics ACh in many ways. ACh effects the entire body from brain cells to muscles and glands. Its purpose is to maintain normal level of function—to maintain balance between all mental and physical body systems. (Figure 2.)

The receptor of ACh does not easily distinguish between acetylcholine and nicotine. So when nicotine enters the nervous system, it increases the level of transmitter substance entering the ACh receptor. The immediate effect is increased ability to concentrate, to work harder, to work faster, to handle stress, to relax, to feel "good" in general. (Figure 3.)

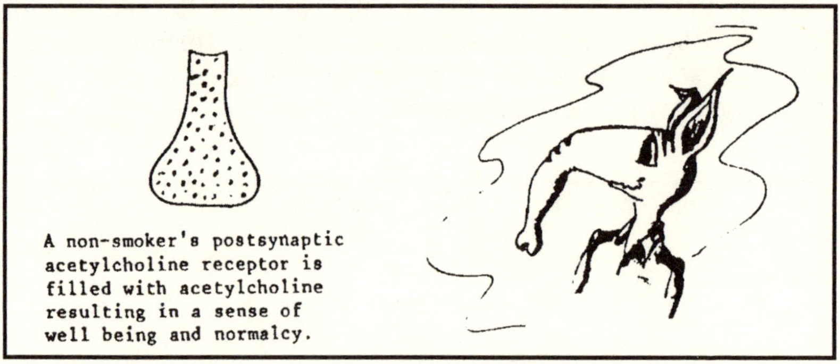

Figure 2.

As the nervous system becomes adapted to nicotine, production of ACh is decreased to "make room for" the nicotine. So, to get all of the good feelings again it is necessary to increase the level of nicotine intake. This is addiction—when the body demands the use of a chemical to maintain the level of function to which one has become adapted.

It generally takes a period of time for addiction to develop and it always takes time to become a non-smoker.

The body does not suddenly start producing sufficient ACh to replace the nicotine withheld. The result is that the ACh receptor is not being fully activated and not only is your addictive level of function gone but the level of function you had prior to smoking has been lowered. You can't concentrate, you feel tired, like you are going at a snail's pace, you aren't handling stress well, you become angered very easily. You may be eating like food is going out of style or you may have an upset stomach. You may have a peculiar taste in your mouth. Remember, your mental, emotional and physical systems are all being affected. In general you do not have a sense of well being. Not everyone reacts to

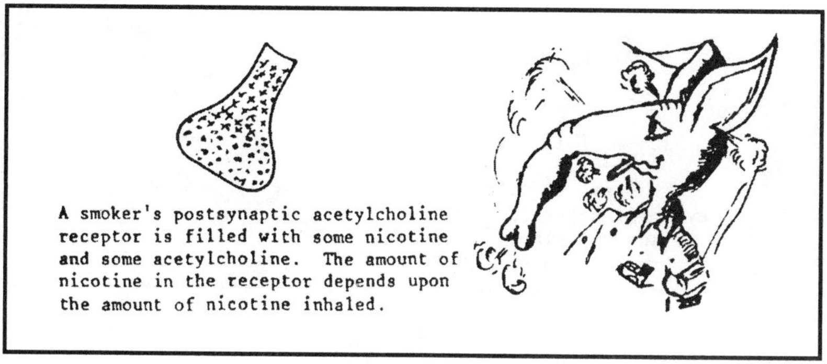

Figure 3.

withdrawal from nicotine in exactly the same way. (Figure 4.)

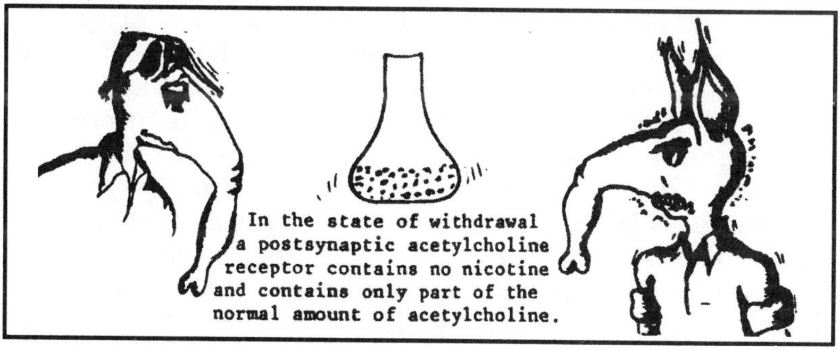

Figure 4.

You might be depressed and, if so, will be until your ACh level of production had returned to normal. The level will be gradually increasing over time and, as a result the depression will be lessening. For some this may take a matter of six to eight weeks. For others it may take as long as six months. (Figure 5.)

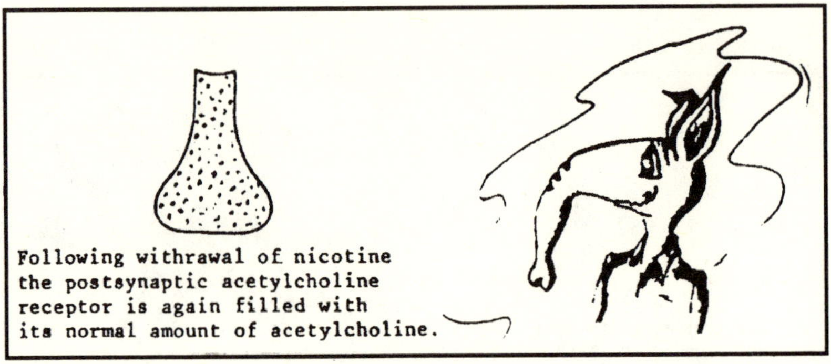

Figure 5.

Depression is by far the worst enemy you might have in attaining your goal of being a non-smoker. Therefore awareness and treatment are of ultimate importance. Your basic program is designed to treat the problem before it becomes severe and incapacitating. Proper diet, a solid exercise program, relaxation and socialization with others who share the goal of non-smoking with you are usually sufficient. With use of "the patch," the total withdrawal of nicotine is not an initial problem, but it may show up when use of the patch is discontinued. However, there is a small percent of individuals withdrawing from nicotine who develop depression which is not controlled by their basic program. If you are in this group, talk to your physician about the problem. He can help you immensely. You do not have to return to smoking to get relief.

With all of the pressures to quit smoking, you've probably wondered "Why do I keep smoking?" You may feel it's hopeless. Or you may unjustifiably feel like you are weak-willed. Or you may believe that since you are addicted, you will never be able to stop smoking anyway.

So let's put the wondering aside and see why you do keep smoking.

3.
WHY YOU CONTINUE SMOKING

"Nobody ever wanted to quit smoking," said co-author Dr. Mary Stevens. "What I really wanted was to get rid of the bad parts of smoking and nicotine. I sure didn't want to quit smoking.

"After fifty years of almost two-pack-a-day smoking I was adamant about continuing to smoke when anyone said anything that resembled a threat to my favorite pastime, my best friend, my constant companion. I knew well that smoking could and probably would cause major health problems and early death. But, when I was confronted with this information by well-meaning (?) friends, my prompt reply was, 'Look, I'm too old to die young, so get off my back.' One thing was certain—the thought of sudden death from a heart attack did not scare me. After all, everyone has to die.

"Sure, I didn't like the way my clothes smelled when I opened the closet. I didn't like my constant sore throat with a raspy voice. I didn't like the hole I had burned in the beautiful new suit I had just bought. I didn't like either having to 'sneak' a cigarette in my office or go outside the building for a smoke on a bitter cold Maine morning when you had to coax the mercury up to zero. I didn't like having to go to the store at midnight when I ran out of cigarettes so I'd be sure to have them first thing in the morning. And I really didn't like paying two dollars a pack. There were a lot of things about smoking I didn't like. Those things are known by many names. I call them results, or negatives. But dying an inch at a time is something I had not really considered.

"While statistics indicate the mortality rate from heart attacks is considerably higher in smokers than non-smokers, the number of sudden deaths from smoking is overshadowed by the number of long, slow, painful deaths from chronic illnesses caused by smoking. With my luck, I wouldn't have a heart attack, but would develop a chronic illness that would rob me of my ability to care for myself. This fact gave me pause to seriously consider what could happen. You see, in my childhood I had made a commitment to myself that I would never live with my children when they were grown and had families of their own. When I realized that I was a physical disaster waiting to happen that would make me violate a lifelong commitment, I made the decision to become a non-smoker."

Becoming a non-smoker is an objective decision. There are clearly identifiable goals to reach and just as clear steps to be taken to reach those goals. To just quit smoking is a subjective decision because you're basing it on emotions and desires that may or may not be carried out. Think about it for a moment . . . if you are thinking about quitting smoking, you are thinking about having to give up something that has become part of your life. Human nature being what it is, no one wants to give up something they enjoy. On the other hand, throughout our lifetime we all attempt to improve ourselves in many ways; for example, how we look, our education, our job and our social lives. So, the thought of "becoming" anything is positive.

If all you want is to quit smoking, close this book now and use it for a bird cage liner. If you're really serious about becoming a non-smoker, keep reading because this program will allow you to clearly outline your steps to get to the end result, and that's being a non-smoker.

4.
AVAILABLE TREATMENT PROGRAMS

Most smokers have tried to "kick the stick" at one time or another. Some are successful, but many more fail. Why the high failure rate? It could be some of the treatments now available are just not extensive enough. The available stop-smoking programs have not been treating the entire problem—only a part of it.

HYPNOSIS

Some smokers try hypnosis to quit. Hypnosis deals with channeling something in your subconscious to a conscious state. But hypnosis demands a high level of motivation as well as effort. What's missing from this method of treatment is the social support follow-up. In other words, there's nobody to help you get through the times when you crave a cigarette. Not everyone can be "put under" by a hypnotist. If you try this method, make sure it's done only by a licensed psychiatrist, psychologist, or social worker that's been accredited by the American Council of Social Work for hypnotherapy treatment.

ACUPUNCTURE

Acupuncture is a relatively new treatment in the Western world. But the Chinese have utilized acupuncture for thousands of years to relieve pains and ailments with some success. The treatment calls for sticking needles into nerve points in the body. The basic idea is to re-route the messages that travel through those nerves. It can be argued that acupuncture may help in relieving the actual physical addiction of a cigarette, but there are no known studies to show that acupuncture stops the smoking habit. And, it doesn't treat the psychological addiction. So, you have to add counseling or a support group program to make acupuncture most effective.

NICOTINE GUM

Nicotine gum is something that's been on the market for a number of years. It's only available by prescription. The gum contains nicotine and is designed to reduce the withdrawal symptoms and allow the smoker to lessen his/her dependence on the need for nicotine. Chewing nicotine gum alone won't help you quit cigarettes. You'll need to get additional help from a support group.

ELECTRIC SHOCK

You could get extreme and get into a rapid smoke and electric shock program. You'll inhale smoke every six seconds until you get sick to your stomach with the rapid smoke program. It's a conditioning program and the basic idea is that you'll associate being nauseated with the act of smoking. There are studies showing it to be very effective. But it's certainly is not everyone's cup of tea. In the electric shock therapy, you get juiced by electric current every time you light up. It's supposed to create an aversion to the behavior, but not the nicotine. And you have to ask yourself; is it really worth it?

GROUP PROGRAMS

Group programs are another way that may help you stop smoking. But they only treat part of the problem—the social-psychological portion. They do nothing for the physical addiction to nicotine.

SELF-HELP

The 1980s were known as the decade of self-help. You could buy books, audio tapes and video cassettes to cure just about any ailment. The jury is still out on whether they really did the job.

All of the programs and treatments mentioned above can work. But, as with hypnosis, they all require constant motivation. And that's something that a lot of people lack. What's more, each of the above programs and treatments addresses either the addiction aspect of smoking or the habit aspect. None treat the whole problem.

NICOTINE PATCH

The nicotine patch that's been making news of late is yet another method and may prove to be the most effective. But for it to be the most effective type of treatment, it has to be used with a human support system. Here's how the nicotine patch works: It's attached to any part of the skin that doesn't have any hair on it. Most people attach it to the upper arm. Others use either side of the upper chest. The patch contains certain drugs and nicotine that are absorbed through the skin by tiny blood vessels near the skin surface. The object of the patch is to provide the body with a constant flow of nicotine, so the craving for a cigarette is eventually gone. The treatment depends on the type of patch that's used, your response to it, and your physician's recommendations. Normally, most people will wear the patch for about six weeks, with the maximum time being three months. Use of the patch for longer than three months may lead to a low-level nicotine addiction. As with any prescription drug, there are some risks, and the patch may not be the answer for you. Your physician can talk about that with you. One thing that is known about the patch: Smoking while wearing it is absolutely forbidden. You could be affected by an overdose of nicotine. Some of the more common prescription patches are Nicoderm, Prostep, Habitrol and Nicotrol.

DO-IT-YOURSELF

And then, there's the "I can do it myself" program. That takes enormous "will power," but we can unequivocally say it won't work.

Think about it for a moment. You're not really doing it by yourself. There is some other action out there that's causing you to pursue this method. For example:

1. Your spouse tells you if you don't quit smoking, he/she is leaving you.
2. You stand to lose your job if you keep smoking.
3. Your physician is constantly telling you to break the smoking habit.
4. You can't smoke in many social settings.

The point is that all of these and many other situations contain another element in your "I can do it myself" program. It's true that you may feel better after a day without a cigarette. However, the following days won't be kind. You need strong support to help you stick to your program of becoming a non-smoker.

5.
THE GOAL-ORIENTED TREATMENT PROGRAM

We're pleased that you decided to make an important decision to keep reading and learning. The light is getting brighter at the end of the tunnel. Once you've completed this program, you'll find that you will have "come a long way, baby."

The treatment program you're about to discover takes the best of all of these various programs and melds it into one that will do far more for you in becoming a permanent non-smoker than anything you have tried.

As you read on, you're probably wondering how long this is going to take. Look, becoming a non-smoker isn't just putting your smokes down and saying "that's it." And it's something that's not going to happen to you overnight. It's a long process that requires you to work to become a non-smoker. How long? That's going to depend largely on you. Take it one step at a time, so you can clearly absorb all of the information. We can't stress the importance of taking enough time with this method. Remember the saying "if it's worth doing, it's worth doing right"? So let's do it right.

GOAL: TO BECOME A PERMANENT NON-SMOKER

Each big step you take to reach your goal is an objective. In the Stevens Non-smoker Program there are three:

A. To understand your physical and behavioral addiction well enough to be able to explain to another person.
B. To tailor your own program to fit your needs.
C. To follow the program you design for yourself.

And for each objective there are the steps that need to be taken to successfully complete that objective . . . something like a recipe.

To get a feel for how you will start let's look at the steps involved in your first objective.

OBJECTIVE A: *To understand your physical and behavioral addiction well enough to be able to explain to another person.*

Step 1. *Keep smoking.* That may sound like an odd way to become a non-smoker. The important thing is that you remain comfortable in what you're doing and are able to concentrate on what you are reading.

Step 2. *Read and re-read all the information about addictions, habits, what nicotine does for you and what it does to you.*

Step 3. *Explain nicotine addiction to your significant other, co-worker or close friend and how that addiction effects people in general.*

That's it for Objective A . . . that is, if your audience of one understood what you were telling him/her. Hopefully you were asked questions and could answer. If not, read and re-read until you thoroughly understand.

OBJECTIVE B: *To write your own treatment plan.*

Step 1. *Establish partnerships.*
Step 2. *Write why you want to become a non-smoker.*
Step 3. *List reasons why you stopped smoking in the past.*
Step 4. *Practice relaxation daily* (Appendix A).
Step 5. *Practice mental imagery daily* (Appendix B).
Step 6. *Make an appointment with your physician for your nicotine patch.*
Step 7. *Plan your diet with your physician or dietician.*
Step 8. *Plan an exercise program with your physician.*
Step 9. *Make a list of self-talk statements.*
Step 10. *Set a start date with your group members.*

You've completed the basic outline of your treatment program. Now let's fill it in with all of the hows, whats and whys.

Step 1 *Establish partnerships*

This program can be successful with just two people working together, but four partners or more would be better. Remember the old adage about strength in numbers? Choose people who have the same goal as you—becoming a non-smoker. Write down their names, addresses and telephone numbers on the worksheet (page) and carry a copy on a card in your pocket or purse. Or, if you're already in a counseling program, talk to the counselor and ask that this program be incorporated into a group format. If you're not in a counseling program now, you don't have to run out and find a suitable one. Your success with becoming a non-smoker with the Stevens Non-smoker Program doesn't hinge on being a part of formal counseling. What it does hinge on is *support.*

Step 2 *Write why you want to become a non-smoker.* You'll be referring back to this list from time to time. Use the worksheet on page 38 for jotting down your thoughts. Put the list where you can readily see it, even if it means you may come across it dozens of times a day. It's important that it be in plain sight. Some of the reasons on your list of why you want to stop smoking may include: health problem or fear of a health problem; family pressure; feeling like a social outcast; etc. You get the idea.

Step 3 *List the reasons why you stopped in the past.* And why you didn't stay a non-smoker. Use the same worksheet on page 38 for your list. Be very honest and specific on this list. Write down how many times you quit and the circumstances surrounding those decisions. Put down on your paper how you quit, whether it was using an existing stop-smoking program, throwing away the pack, or whatever the case was. Add to that the situations and people involved when you chose to start smoking again. This is a very important step that will identify past triggers for lighting up again. Be aware of them and plan ways of avoiding these same triggers in the future.

Step 4 *Practice relaxation daily.* Turn to Appendix A. Follow the instructions carefully, and in no time you will be able to relax "at the snap of a finger." You will be using relaxation for countering an urge to light up, for keeping your cool when you would like to kick the dog, yell at your kids, and stomp out of the room to go find a cigarette. You will also be using this for mental imagery.

Step 5 *Practice mental imagery daily.*

Turn to Appendix B for instructions. We'll show you how to become totally relaxed and build a picture in your mind of what it will be like to be a non-smoker. You'll also see a picture in your mind of you refusing an offer of a cigarette. Mental imagery will require practice but you will find it very rewarding.

Step 6 *Make an appointment with your physician for your nicotine patch.*

This is a critical step in your plan. The patch will either minimize or prevent strong urges to smoke while you are learning to change behaviors associated with smoking. With a great deal on our minds we sometimes tend to forget details that could be important. Therefore, it is suggested that you write the instructions on the worksheet on page 40 for ready reference.

Step 7 *Plan your diet with the assistance of your physician or a dietician.*

Because of the physical changes occurring in becoming a non-smoker, your body will not burn its "fuel" as rapidly as when you were smoking and you will probably gain some weight. The normal weight gain with proper dietary intake and exercise averages between five and seven pounds. With no dietary controls, the weight can become a problem. Incidentally, excess weight gain has been the excuse numerous smokers have given for returning to smoking. If you are looking for excuses and are not truly motivated to become a non-smoker, this one will do. On the other hand, if you are motivated, plan your diet. Write it on your diet plan worksheet, page 41.

Step 8 *Plan an exercise program.*

Ask your physician or a physical therapist to help you with this. Obviously the exercise will work along with your diet in weight control. But there is a lot more to it than that. Exercise helps your body produce "endorphins," which produce a natural "high." Another thing to consider is that exercise for exercise sake is usually rather boring and soon forgotten. So you might consider exercise such as swimming, hiking, dancing and other fun activities with other people.

Step 9 *Make a list of self-talk statements.*

You no doubt talk to yourself at times. Everyone does. And the way you talk to yourself has a definite effect on your self confidence. You're going to need to develop a list of positive "self-talk" statements to support your new found non-smoking behavior. Use the worksheet on page 43. What you want to do is reinforce yourself with statements of fact about why you don't want a cigarette when you suddenly get that urge to smoke. You want to do it in a positive manner. You might say to yourself that you don't want a cigarette because your breath will smell like smoke. Or, you might say to yourself that you won't smoke because you don't want your clothes to have the stench of cigarette smoke. Another positive statement would be that "this urge to smoke is the addiction talking, not me . . . and I'm in charge of myself."

Step 10 *Set a start date* with your group members.

Now comes the big decision. When do you want to become a non-smoker? Plan the start date far enough in advance to give all of you time to make your appointments, write your treatment plans, learn relaxation and mental imagery, and meet regularly to share your progress. You and your buddies have to do this together. The entire group has to agree on the start date. This is because if you're not all on the same bus, so to speak, you won't be able to identify things that are happening. If you stop a week before your "buddies," you'll have different experiences that will be difficult for everyone to relate to. Usually, six to eight weeks after you've started meeting with your buddies is good.

You have completed writing your own program, tailored to your personal needs, and it's a plan that you can understand and follow. After all, you gave birth to it. So let's look and see what you can do and how you can do it to make the most of your program.

Remembering all of the information and details in your ten-step program may seem overwhelming at first. That is why you have worksheets to jog your memory. And, we repeat, do just one step at a time.

OBJECTIVE C: *To follow the program you designed for yourself.*

Step 1

During your first meeting with your group of buddies, make a decision about when, where, and how often you will meet. Initially, meeting twice a week is recommended. While you are in the active learning and starting part of this program, sharing thoughts, questions and ideas about your treatment plans is extremely important. You won't need to meet this often later in the program. As you all decide the best place to meet, be sure to consider the need for a place where you can smoke. Remember, you are to continue smoking while you are learning and planning.

Step 2

At this first meeting (after you have set meeting details) talk with the others about your reasons for wanting to become a non-smoker. Everybody has their own reasons. Still, you might find that you have some of the same reasons someone else has. Then, before you meet the next time, complete the worksheet on page 38. During the second meeting you and your buddy(ies) review your worksheets together. Then proceed to the next list . . . reasons you stopped smoking in the past, how often and why, and why you started smoking again. Talk this over with the others and before the next meeting complete the "Trigger" worksheet, page 39. You will be identifying some of the very reasons you were not successful in your past efforts to stop smoking. You will be discussing this at your next meeting.

Step 3

Meetings will continue on a regular basis, each meeting being a time and place to share the problems or progress you have experienced since the last meeting. You can start learning relaxation techniques any time you choose. Read Appendix A and follow the instructions. At first you may think nothing is happening. But after some practice you will find you can relax very quickly and completely. The sooner you learn this, the longer you will have to learn it well before you really need it in the business of becoming a non-smoker. Practicing a minimum of once a day (and more often when time is available) is suggested.

Step 4

The same thing applies to mental imagery. Once you have learned relaxation methods, begin using mental imagery. At first it may feel a bit awkward. After you have practiced a while, it becomes second nature.

Step 5

When you make an appointment with your physician is optional. You may prefer to do it as you start this program. Or you may prefer to wait until it is closer to the "Start Date." Just remember, you are going to see him not only for a prescription and instructions for the nicotine patch, but for his input and suggestions regarding exercise and diet. The earlier in the program that you make this appointment and get your physician's recommendations, the longer you have to set up and use an exercise and diet routine before you actually withdraw from nicotine. Be sure to write your nicotine patch instructions on page 40, exercise program on page 42, and diet plan on page 41.

Step 6

Writing your list of "self-talk statements" (on the worksheet on page 43) is a task where input from your "groupies" might help . . . might give you some ideas. Think about all the reasons you don't want to pick up that cigarette, then write some of them into statements that you memorize and say to yourself when you get that urge to smoke.

Step 7

Setting your "S-Day" is a big event that should happen in six to eight weeks after group meetings have started.

Your work is cut out for you after you've set your "S-Day." First, gradually cut back on the number of cigarettes you smoke. For example, if you're a two-pack-a-day smoker, reduce that number to one pack. If you smoke only one pack of cigarettes a day, cut that number in half. Buy only one pack of cigarettes at a time and keep your lighter or matches with that pack and not with you. There are basically two reasons why you should cutback on the cigarettes before "S-Day." The first is that you'll start to change your behavior around smoking. Reason number two is because the higher the nicotine concentration in your system prior to halting smoking, the greater the urge for a cigarette during the early weeks of not smoking.

Next, reduce the number of ashtrays around the house and office to only one.

A couple of days before "S-Day" arrives, refer back to the list you made about why you stopped smoking in the past and didn't stay stopped. You may find that the list has to be updated. If so, make any necessary changes. And remember, be completely honest with yourself.

The absolute last thing to do before "S-Day" arrives is to meet with your partners in a social setting and snuff out that last cigarette. Consider it as a ceremony of sorts. Go ahead, light up as many times as you want. But when that last butt is put out, all of you need to take your packs of cigarettes, your lighters or matches, and dump them into the nearest trash can.

6.
"S-DAY" IS HERE!

The day that you've been waiting for has finally arrived! It's the dawn of a new day in your life. You've learned new ways to deal with life without a cigarette. Now it's time to put all that you've learned into practice. After today is over and done with, you'll be a part of the growing ranks of non-smokers around the world.

Get up and enjoy life! Take a walk around the house. There aren't any cigarette packages littering the trash. The stinky ashtrays are gone. You're on your way to a new beginning.

After getting up, remember to start your day with that diet you and your physician set up. We've always been told that starting the day with an honest-to-goodness breakfast goes a long way toward helping you get off to a good day. There's a lot of truth to that. By eating a good, cholesterol-free breakfast, you'll be priming the metabolic burner in you. In other words, you'll have much more energy from the glucose contained in the breakfast to face the rigors of the day. Also, since your brain works the best in the morning hours you're craving for a cigarette will be greatly inhibited. You won't need a "rush" to get going. If you're a caffeine drinker, eliminate it from your diet. Substitute caffeine-free products. Caffeine is also a stimulant that works hand-in-hand with nicotine.

After getting ready to meet the day head on, fill your pockets with the hard candies or sugarless gum you bought before "S-Day" arrived. These candies or gum are really necessary. They'll give your mouth and hands something to do when you crave a cigarette. If you elect to use hard candies, they will provide a substantive amount of glucose for your brain power. That glucose is going to replace the nicotine that used to supply that "fuel" for thinking. The sugarless gum will merely keep your hands and mouth occupied.

If you drive to your workplace, you'll find that the car does, indeed, start and actually move without being powered by nicotine. If you use public transportation to get to the workplace, you'll discover that it still arrives without you having to light up. If you're in a rideshare program, inform your rideshare partners that you've embarked on a new voyage—that of being a non-smoker. You might be surprised at the support you get from them.

You've made it to the workplace. If you're the typical smoker, you'll come across a number of situations where you'll be looking for a cigarette. Those could include, but are not limited to, whenever you have to talk on the telephone, the boss calls you in for a meeting, another smoker comes into your office, or you have a cup of decaffeinated coffee. How do you handle these situations?

If you're wearing a nicotine patch, most of the physical craving won't appear. That will help.

If you have properly prepared for "S-Day," these cravings probably will be minimal. Moreover, if you told your co-workers about your being a non-smoker (and you should have) they're not about to become a co-conspirator and ruin your best chance to become a non-smoker.

But if the urge hits you with a vengeance, here's how you can keep your sanity. Immediately reach for a piece of the hard candy or sugarless gum you brought with you and pop it in your mouth. Also, grab the nearest pen or pencil to keep your hands busy. Go ahead, you can hold it like a cigarette, it's okay. Remember the list you made on why you wanted to be a non-smoker? You should have a copy of that with you and anytime the urge for a cigarette hits you, pull out that list and look it over. This is one of the best ways to condition yourself to be a non-smoker.

Then there is relaxation and mental imagery to deflate that urge.

You can relax at your desk, in the lunch room, even in your car (but it would be a good idea to keep your eyes open if you're the driver). Deep relaxation and thoughts of being a non-smoker take but a minute or two and destroy the immediate urge.

There's no telling how many times a day the urge to smoke will consume you. It depends on how much you used to smoke and/or how addicted to cigarettes you've become. For some people, the urge may happen every five minutes. Some may not experience the urge for a half hour. Still others may find the urge striking on the hour. And there are those non-smokers who may find the urge doesn't really strike them at all. The bottom line is that everyone is different.

Another way to lose the urge to smoke is maintain contact with your support group. Give them a call and talk about your urge. Chances are they're going through the same problem and together you can work it out. It's important to remember now that you're not dealing with the craving for nicotine. If you're wearing a patch, that craving is being minimized. We're talking about the psychological aspects of the smoking habit.

You've gotten through the workday without smoking. Feel pretty good, right? There's no reason why that good feeling can't continue. If you drive yourself home from work, remember that the car got you there this morning without you having to smoke a cigarette. It can get you home in the same fashion. However, you'll be presented with another set of circumstances once you get home—no cigarette after dinner or before bed. What do you do?

Being at home presents you with the greatest opportunity to change your conditioned behavior from being a smoker to a non-smoker. If you're one who comes home from work and reads the newspaper while smoking a cigarette, try watching the television instead (without the cigarette, of course). If you watch television, read the newspaper or a book. If you're the cook and usually have a halo of smoke surrounding you while coming up with your latest culinary delight, you might consider trying some frozen dinners for a couple of days. Those don't take as long to prepare, so fewer opportunities are presented to smoke.

After dinner, don't sit around the table and talk. Instead, go for a walk with your favorite person or pet (unless your pet is a cat, fish or bird, since they don't go on walks very well). You'll not only burn up energy while on the walk, you'll also burn up time you used to allot for smoking. If taking a walk is not possible because of where you reside or a physical limitation, pick up a favorite book and occupy your time. Don't forget to touch base with your support group. All of you have gone through your first day as non-smokers and you have a lot to talk about. You'll be able to help them with any problems they may have encountered, and, they'll be able to assist you as well.

Earlier, we mentioned that a good exercise program is part and parcel of your success with this stop-smoking program. An exercise program is extremely important for both your physical and mental well-being. You should have consulted with your physician about setting up a sound exercise program before embarking on the program. If you need to exercise on a daily basis, don't forget to do so. Some people are able to handle an exercise program better in the morning, right after they rise. Others are better equipped to get more out of their workout later in the day or in the evening. Whatever your particular case, don't forget to exercise.

If you're person who likes to exercise in the evening, you're in a better position to not smoke before bedtime. You've used up a lot of energy and the last thing you want to do is light up a smoke. Whether or not you exercise before bedtime, make sure you brush your teeth. The taste of toothpaste is surely much better than the taste of a cigarette. If you have a bedtime partner, we can pretty much guarantee they'll appreciate you more with the fresh taste of toothpaste as opposed the dank odor of cigarette smoke.

Now, go to bed and congratulate yourself. You've just made it through your first day as a non-smoker!

7. STAYING A NON-SMOKER

Day One as a non-smoker was okay, right? Face it, you really didn't miss having a cigarette, did you? Oh well, at least your clothes weren't permeated with the smell of smoke. The inside of your vehicle wasn't all trashed up with cigarette butts. The "fog" in your house or apartment has lifted. And, your overall personality didn't suffer because you didn't smoke yesterday. If anything, your personality is starting to improve.

If Day One was that great, can Day Two match? What about Day Three and Day Four and so on? Yes, and succeeding days will get even better. The reason and strategy is quite simple. You'll be repeating everything you did on Day One for the rest of your days as a non-smoker. In other words, you'll be developing new habits—ones that will keep you off cigarettes.

There will be some exceptions, though. After at least four weeks following "S-Day," daily contact with your support group won't be necessary. That's not to say if you need to talk with the group, you can't. But after that four-week period, all of you will have developed your routines. You will, however, want to meet with the group a minimum of once a week. After six months, you and the group can determine how often you need to meet.

We do have a warning that you need to heed. It's liable to come up at anytime from after the first week you've become a non-smoker to maybe twenty-five years after you've developed a new lease on life. There will come a time (probably when you least expect it) that you'll think it's okay to have "just one" cigarette. It could happen when you are socializing with friends, going out dancing, eating at a fancy restaurant, simply smelling the smoke of a cigarette or whatever. So, let's say, you have that cigarette and find that in a very short time you're back in the full swing of smoking just as though you'd never stopped. What happened? The nicotine in that one cigarette went right to those ACh receptors we talked about earlier . . . and your addiction said "ahhhh". You see, addictions are never "cured." They are just controlled by not providing your body with the drug of choice. Your nervous system is what's more or less in control here. It can't tell time and doesn't know if you're on Week One of being a non-smoker or you're in you're twenty-fifth year without a cigarette. Taking nicotine into your system, even after twenty-five years, would immediately start the physical addiction again. So, the important thing to keep in mind here is that this urge is a psychological one, not a physical one. How do you handle this urge?

Because you'll be able to recognize that this urge is psychological and not physical, you'll be able to stop and ask yourself, "Do I really want to smoke this cigarette?" The answer should be a resounding "NO!" Why would you want to go back to the nagging cough that accompanied your smoking, the smell of smoke in your clothes, your house and your car. Not only that, but think about all the money you've saved from not smoking and the fact that you won't ever again have to empty your purse or pockets looking for a lighter or matches.

Sometime back, you made the choice to become a non-smoker. It won't hurt to go back and review your reasons.

In fact, reviewing those all-important reasons will allow you to remain a non-smoker for the rest of your days.

One final note: At first you may feel out of place because you've made the choice to become a non-smoker. That's because you really don't know how to act . . . it's been so long since you were a non-smoker. That doesn't mean you have to be asocial. Current figures indicate twenty-five percent of the adult population in this country are smokers. You'll be joining a good crowd, the seventy-five percent non-smokers. So hang in there, socialize at first with your non-smoking buddies, then branch out to enjoy yourself with other friends. Unlike the situation when you were a smoker, there's not a single social event that you cannot attend or be involved in because you are a non-smoker. The more you enjoy life as a non-smoker, the more you will want to stay with it. So enjoy your new life.

"REASONS" WORKSHEET

List all of your reasons for becoming a non-smoker. After you have finished writing your list, rewrite the reasons on a card you can carry in your pocket or purse. Be sure to write your major motivation at the top of the list.

1. ______________________________
2. ______________________________
3. ______________________________
4. ______________________________
5. ______________________________
6. ______________________________
7. ______________________________
8. ______________________________
9. ______________________________
10. ______________________________
11. ______________________________
12. ______________________________

"TRIGGER" WORKSHEET

1. How many times have you tried to quit smoking? ____

2. On each occasion, how long did you remain non-smoking?
   1st____ 2nd____ 3rd____ 4th____ 5th____
   6 or more____

3. What happened that you returned to smoking on each of these occasions? Be sure to include the time, place, persons involved and specific situation. It is very important that you identify each set of events. These were the triggers that started you smoking again in the past. Now that you recognize the triggers, you can make plans to avoid these situations or learn new ways of handling them. If you do not have enough room on this sheet, use a blank worksheet and insert after last line below.

____
____
____
____
____
____
____

DOCTOR'S INSTRUCTIONS FOR THE "PATCH"

DIET PLAN

EXERCISE PLAN

SELF-TALK STATEMENTS

These are statements to be used whenever I have a strong urge to smoke:

1. (example) The urge is temporary. This too shall pass.
2. (example) This craving is the addiction screaming, not what my mind wants. I won't give in to it.
3.
4.
5.
6.
7.
8.
9.
10.

APPENDIX A
RELAXATION METHODS

Why: Intentional "relaxation" is a skill that will permit you to immediately relax physically in response to your mental desire or verbal statement "relax." When you have practiced and honed your skills, all of your muscles will respond in unison to the command "relax."

When: The very best time to learn how to relax is when you are wide awake and alert. Your mind is better able to "pay attention" to details. Once you have learned these methods you will be able to use them successfully at any time of day or night . . . when you feel stressed out or when you can't get to sleep. For now, the main reasons for learning relaxation methods are to be able to relax when you have a craving for a cigarette and to use mental imagery.

Where: A quiet place where you will not be disturbed for 20 minutes at a time will provide the perfect atmosphere for learning. After you have learned, you can "relax" in a crowded room, at your desk at the office, in a restaurant, or even after an argument that would usually result in a headache.

How: Sit in your easy chair or lounger. Any chair with arms will do, but the more comfortable you are, the better . . . that is, in a sitting position. While you may use relaxation as a means of getting to sleep later, the idea now is not to get to sleep, but to stay awake, to actively learn how to relax. Now that you are sitting, loosen any tight clothes like a tie or your belt; put both feet flat on the floor in front of you; rest your arms on the chair arms, and *do not* put your head back on a head rest.

You will be working with muscle groups. As you tighten each set of muscles and then relax them, you will feel a tingling sensation for a moment. This is as it should be. The most important part of each of these exercises is to *think* and *say to yourself RELAX* as you are actually relaxing each set of muscles.

First, the face. Work every muscle in your face forcefully . . . pull you eyebrows together, close your eyes very tightly, wrinkle your nose, smile the biggest smile possible, then take a deep breath and drop your jaw to your neck with your mouth open. To do this, your head will be erect and the back of your neck will feel stretched. Hold it for a count of ten seconds. Then exhale and let all of those face muscles go loose. Feel the tingle?

Next, go to the arms. Make very tight fists; hold both arms straight out at shoulder height; sitting erect, take a deep breath, tighten the muscles in both arms, both shoulders and your neck. Hold for a count of ten, then let those muscles become loose. Are you remembering to think and say "relax" as you relax each muscle group?

Throw your shoulders back, chest out, and take a very slow, deep breath, pushing your diaphragm muscle out. Hold your breath for ten seconds and exhale slowly. Repeat this twice before going on.

Now, throw your shoulders forward, head down, cross your arms tightly across your chest, lean forward to stretch your back muscles until they feel tight. Hold this position for ten seconds, then slowly sit up straight.

While pulling your stomach in, tighten your waist as far as possible. You naturally take a big breath in when you do this. After holding your breath the usual ten seconds, exhale slowly.

You're sitting on the next set of muscles you'll work with. Slide your feet slightly forward on the floor, then tighten your "maximus gluteus muscles" and your upper thighs. Hold these as tight as you can for at least twenty seconds. These are very large muscles that play an important part in your being able to relax.

The last group of muscles are those of your feet and lower legs. Hold them straight out (or as near as possible) in front of you, pull the toes straight up and then toward you, then tightening your knees, point your toes forward and hold for at least ten seconds. Put your feet back on the floor.

Now you may rest your head on the headrest of your chair. All of your muscles have been relaxed and you feel good. Go ahead and close your eyes for a few minutes and savor being truly relaxed.

These exercises take considerable time, as you are learning. But once you have paired the word "relax" with the act of relaxing many times, your body will cooperate with your mind and you will be able to become completely relaxed by saying "relax" to yourself.

APPENDIX B
MENTAL IMAGERY

Mental imagery is very much like daydreaming, except that the thoughts are not idle dreams; rather, they are a series of images guided by your mind. For that matter, this is sometimes called "guided imagery."

There are two reasons for you to learn mental imagery. The first is to experience the positive feelings of being nicotine-free. This is a strong motivating factor in the process of becoming a non-smoker. The second reason is to experience situations of the past in which you returned to smoking, and "re-play" the scene with you now avoiding taking that cigarette. This helps prepare you mentally for using some of the methods you have learned for not falling into traps.

So much for what we are going to do. Let's do it.

The first step is to get in a comfortable position, completely relax and close your eyes. Again, it is better to not be lying down, since you might drift off to sleep.

You can take short jaunts or long excursions into the land of "No Nicotine." With your eyes closed, imagine going into the store to buy a gallon of milk and walking right past the cigarette counter. You don't need to buy that carton of cigarettes. Wow, you just saved a tidy sum. Feels good, doesn't it, especially when it's the day before payday. This was one of the thirty-second mental jaunts.

You will be able to imagine opening up your closet door and your clothes won't smell of smoke. You'll also be able to picture your clothes without burn marks from dropped ashes. Telephone conversations will be done without a cigarette in your free hand. It's so much easier to pay attention to the other side of the conversation that way. Picture yourself driving your car as a non-smoker. You'll be able to concentrate on the road instead of hitting the ashtray with the cigarette. Your car's interior won't have that smoky odor either. You might imagine what it will be like in social settings where you won't have to worry if smoking is allowed. You'll also be able to imagine not smoking at home with that guilty feeling that your second-hand smoke is a health hazard for your loved ones. One other image you might think about is the money in the bank that you have saved not having to buy cigarettes and with the reduced premium for your "non-smoking driver" status. If you've ever seen the movie "It's a Wonderful Life," you know that the main character had a chance to see what life was like without him. You're doing the same thing, basically. You are imagining what life is like being a non-smoker. And, very soon, your imagination with this will become reality.

It's time now to refer back to your worksheet for "triggers." Here you will find a list of the situations in which you gave up your non-smoker status and picked up that cigarette. As you review it you will see a mental picture of the whole scene, i.e. where you were, who was there, what happened, etc. Think about what you could do now in the same situation to have a different ending. You might also use one or more of your "self-talk" statements.

You have decided to use the scene when you went out to dinner with a friend who was a smoker. Of course, out of courtesy to your dinner companion, you sat in the smoking section. You ordered drinks while you waited for your dinner. Then he/she casually offered you a cigarette. You accepted.

With the knowledge you have now of why you have kept on smoking, the triggers that set you off, and things you can do about it, live that scene over in a way that will let you be a winner. Get comfortable, relax and close your eyes. See yourself and your partner talking about going out to dinner. Since you know he/she is a smoker, you let it be known that you are becoming a non-smoker and would appreciate sitting in the non-smoking section of the restaurant. There are no ashtrays, matches, or other people smoking to give you that urge. If, in the past, you have always had a cigarette with a cocktail, you will skip the cocktail for the time being. And, as your friend suggests going to the lounge while waiting for dinner, and out of habit, offers you a cigarette, you will silently use one of your self-talk statements such as "I want to really become a non-smoker this time" and graciously refuse.

As you practice refusing a cigarette through the replay of scenes using positive endings, you will find that refusal becomes much easier.

Mental imagery might sound "hokey" to you at first. Just remember it is a tried and true technique that will let you practice acting in the manner to which you would like to become accustomed.

ADDENDUM

"So," you are saying to yourself, "I've read your whole book and have done what it said. Now sixteen weeks later, I'm smoking! What happened and what do I do?"

You didn't reach your goal of becoming a non-smoker because you didn't complete all of your objectives. You either missed or omitted one or more of the steps. Cutting corners in this program doesn't speed up the process. It either slows it down or stops it completely.

So, go back and start checking your three major objectives and each of the steps involved. Put a check mark in front of each step listed below that you completed.

Did you keep smoking during the time you were reading, learning and developing the details of your program? Hopefully, you didn't jump the gun and stop before "S-Day." That's a surefire set up for starting to smoke again before you have learned how to not smoke.

Did you fully understand your physical and behavioral addiction well enough to be able to explain to another individual? If not, talk the explanations over with your partner(s). They can help. It is much easier to treat and solve any problem when you understand what the problem is.

Did you establish a partnership or group and meet with them as recommended? One of the biggest pitfalls is that old thinking of "I can do it myself. I don't need other people to help." Even if you did form that partnership or group and did not meet with them frequently and regularly, you did not have the support you needed to gain non-smoking status.

What about each of your written assignments? Did you feel it wasn't necessary to write down all that "stuff" since you had all of it in your head? Well, you've known all this before and haven't stopped smoking. The more of our senses we use in learning anything, the better we learn it. By writing down thoughts, you are then reading them. By talking them over with your buddies, you are then speaking and hearing the thoughts. Your sense of touch has been involved in writing them. All of that information that was just floating around in your head now becomes knowledge to be used in changing behaviors.

If you chose not to use the nicotine patch, you have made becoming a non-smoker more difficult than it need be.

If you did see your physician for the "patch," did you write his/her instructions on your work sheet? It's so easy to forget details, especially when you are making a major change in your life.

Did you develop a diet plan for yourself and then *follow it?* If you omitted this step and immediately gained weight, you may have subconsciously made the decision to return to smoking rather than "get fat."

Hand in hand with a diet plan, did you write and follow an exercise plan? When you exercise, your body produces "endorphins," the body's own natural drug that creates a "high." Not only does exercise help control your weight, but it also gives you considerable energy that aids in preventing depression.

Which step(s) did you find that you had either omitted or short cut? That's what you need to go back and do. And as you are carrying this out, be absolutely sure you have a strong support system.

IF YOU ARE MOTIVATED TO BECOME A NON-SMOKER, YOU CAN DO IT.

REFERENCES

1. Ashton, H., and Stepney, R. "The Indians' Revenge: A Brief History of the Tobacco Habit and its Current Status," in *Smoking: Psychology and Pharmacology*. London: Tavistock, 1982, pp. 1–17.
2. "The Health Consequences of Smoking: Nicotine Addiction. A Report of the Surgeon General." Rockville, Md. Centers for Disease Control, Office of Smoking and Health, 1988.
3. "Reducing the Health Consequences of Smoking: 25 Years of Progress. A Report of the Surgeon General." U.S. Department of Health and Human Services, Centers for Disease Control, Center for Chronic Disease Prevention and Health Promotion, Office on Smoking and Health. DHHS Publication no. CDC 89-8411.
4. "Psychoactive Substance Abuse Disorders." Diagnostic and Statistical Manual of Mental Disorders, Third Edition, Revised. American Psychiatric Association, Washington, D.C. 1987, pp. 165–170.
5. Olendorf, W.H. "Distribution of Drugs to the Brain." In M.E. Jarvik, ed., *Psychopharmacology in the Practice of Medicine*. New York: Appleton-Century-Crofts, 1977, pg. 167.
6. Neher, T.L. "Altered (Chemical) States: A Practical Look at Brain Chemistry and Addictions." *Professional Counselor,* Mar/Apr 1991.

7. Russell, M.A.H. "Tobacco Smoking and Nicotine Dependence." In R.J. Gibbins et al., eds. *Research Advances in Alcohol and Drug Problems,* Vol. 3, New York: Wiley, 1976.
8. Blum, K. "Tobacco and Smoking Behavior." In *Handbook of Abusable Drugs.* New York: Gardner Press, 1992.
9. "How to Quit Smoking Using Nicoderm." Patient Instructions. Marion Merrell Dow, Inc., Kansas City, Missouri, 1992.
10. "Habitrol (nicotine transermal system)." Patient Instructions. Basel Pharmaceuticals, Division of Ciba-Geigy Corporation. Summit, New Jersey, 1992.
11. "Prostep (nicotine transdermal system)." Patient Information. Lederle Laboratories. Division of American Cyanamid Company. Pearl River, New York, 1992.
12. "Nicotrol (nicotine transdermal system)." Information sheet. Parke-Davis. A Warner-Lambert Company. Morris Plains, NJ, 1992.